Language Walk-through for Very Busy People

by Hermann M. Hess

R Language Walk-through for Very Busy People

First Edition

Paintings - "Carnival" (Title page) and "Fantasy" (Dedication page) by Hermann M. Hess

First published: July 2019

Dedication

With love for Aura Violeta,
Mauricio and Xinjun,
Federico and Marcela,
and little Victoria.

Preface

Welcome to *R Language Walk-through for Very Busy People*. This book was written with you in mind, so that you can quickly progress towards a more advanced knowledge of **R** and its environment.

Whether you are just curious or taking your first steps towards mastering the **R** programming world, this book will show you the basic **R** landmarks; allowing you to start wandering about this terrain with confidence and sense of direction. It is not meant to be an exhaustive technical manual but a basic map that will help you explore the landscape and get a general feel of what **R** can do.

This has implied a fairly lop-sided chapter length approach – greater conceptual fluidity suggested a lengthier chapter dedicated to basic concepts, in contrast to those that focus on more specific skills such as data, graphics, time series and programming. This of course does not mean that you have to do it all in one sitting - there are sections and topics that further divide this relatively protracted chapter and allow you to progress at a customized pace.

R has a reputation of leading you up a steep learning curve, but it doesn't have to be that way. This book will take you from sea level to many of **R**'s challenging mountain ranges, without making the experience an exhausting *tour de force*. This of course requires a minimum of training and fitness, so please do follow the examples in your **R** installation as we advance in the book. This minimal practice will provide a very solid foundation, necessary to master the tools required by more extensive and complex applications you will encounter in 'real life'.

But let's not exaggerate either - many powerful calculations and visualizations can be accomplished in **R** without the need for '*more extensive and complex applications*'. As you will see, in many instances a few lines of **R** code manage to solve substantial problems - that's a big part of **R**'s appeal. Hopefully, this book will help you quickly feel at home in your new niche in the **R** ecosystem.

Table of Contents

Introduction

What is R?

R is basically a computation and data visualization environment which is a prominent player in today's life and physical sciences, statistics, econometrics, finance, data science and many other domains. It is simple enough to be used as a desktop calculator but at the same time capable of easily handling complex and very large amounts of data, such as the ones that machine learning algorithms love to gobble up.

The **R** programming language was developed by Ross Ihaka and Robert Gentleman at the University of Auckland, New Zealand, in the mid 90s as a shoot-off from the S Language, developed in turn by John Chambers in 1976, while at Bell Labs, as a statistical and general computing environment.

Although it has been around for some time, the advent of data science brought it to the foreground because of its many advantages in this specialized context. Even though it is not a general programming language in the sense of Python or Java, it ranks among the top ten or twenty languages in popularity indexes such as Tiobe, PyPl or Redmonk.

R is huge - there is a core component that handles all the fundamental data input-output, numerical and text operations, and graphics. But this central engine room is complemented by over 14.000 packages (as of this writing) that ride on top of this core and carry out thousands of domain-specific tasks and calculations.

There are packages for everything:

Bayesian Inference
Chemometrics and Computational Physics
Clinical Trial Design, Monitoring, and Analysis
Cluster Analysis & Finite Mixture Models
Databases with R
Differential Equations

Probability Distributions
Econometrics
Analysis of Ecological and Environmental Data
Design of Experiments (DoE) & Analysis of Experimental Data
Extreme Value Analysis
Empirical Finance
Functional Data Analysis
Statistical Genetics
Graphic Displays & Dynamic Graphics & Graphic Devices
High-Performance and Parallel Computing with R
Hydrological Data and Modeling
Machine Learning & Statistical Learning
Medical Image Analysis
Meta-Analysis
Missing Data
Model Deployment with R
Multivariate Statistics
Natural Language Processing
Numerical Mathematics
Official Statistics & Survey Methodology
Optimization and Mathematical Programming
Analysis of Pharmacokinetic Data
Phylogenetics, Especially Comparative Methods
Psychometric Models and Methods
Reproducible Research
Robust Statistical Methods
Statistics for the Social Sciences
Analysis of Spatial Data
Handling and Analyzing Spatio-Temporal Data
Survival Analysis
Teaching Statistics
Time Series Analysis
Web Technologies and Services
gRaphical Models in R

Plus of course all the mathematical and statistical stuff (optimization, linear algebra, numerical integration and differentiation, statistical models, plots, etc.) that's already there in basic **R**.

Want to add 2 and 2? No problem! Want to estimate a recurrent neural network model with 25 features and 1.000 epochs? No problem either, there's a package for that (but it will take longer than 2 and 2!). Quants will be happy downloading and modeling financial data while others develop geospatial models; but there's also room for someone who just wants to summarize their data and construct a very nice publication-quality plot. In any case, our exploration of **R** will be general and basic, so there will be no need for specialized, technical or domain-specific knowledge.

Assumptions About Computer Knowledge

This book assumes that you already know how to deal with the basics of computer use and terminology. Although we will begin with the process of installation of a suitable **R** programming environment, it is assumed that you know how to perform basic computer tasks such as exploring files, saving, and Cut and Paste. Also, that you have a basic understanding of things such as 'bits', 'bytes', RAM memory and use of the Internet.

A modern 'normal' desktop or laptop computer shall be more than enough to comply with this book's basic **R** software and hardware requirements.

Assumptions About Programming

Although familiarity with a programming language such as Java or Python is an asset, this book assumes that you are not a programmer and that you will here learn the basics of things such as *'for'* loops, *'functions'* or *'conditional statements'*.

Download and install R and RStudio

This is an easy two-stage process. This illustration will be carried out with the Windows version.

First, download **R** from https://cran.r-project.org/ .

The Comprehensive R Archive Network

Download and Install R

Precompiled binary distributions of the base system and contributed packages, **Windows and Mac** users most likely want one of these versions of R:

- Download R for Linux
- Download R for (Mac) OS X
- Download R for Windows

R is part of many Linux distributions, you should check with your Linux package management system in addition to the link above.

Source Code for all Platforms

Windows and Mac users most likely want to download the precompiled binaries listed in the upper box, not the source code. The sources have to be compiled before you can use them. If you do not know what this means, you probably do not want to do it!

- The latest release (2019-04-26, Planting of a Tree) R-3.6.0.tar.gz, read what's new in the latest version.

- Sources of R alpha and beta releases (daily snapshots, created only in time periods before a planned release).

- Daily snapshots of current patched and development versions are available here. Please read about new features and bug fixes before filing corresponding feature requests or bug reports.

- Source code of older versions of R is available here.

- Contributed extension packages

CRAN
Mirrors
What's new?
Task Views
Search

About R
R Homepage
The R Journal

Software
R Sources
R Binaries
Packages
Other

Documentation
Manuals
FAQs
Contributed

Choose the **base** or basic version:

R for Windows

Subdirectories:

base	Binaries for base distribution. This is what you want to **install R for the first time**.
contrib	Binaries of contributed CRAN packages (for R >= 2.13.x; managed by Uwe Ligges). There is also services and corresponding environment and make variables.
old contrib	Binaries of contributed CRAN packages for outdated versions of R (for R < 2.13.x; managed by U
Rtools	Tools to build R and R packages. This is what you want to build your own packages on Windows,

Please do not submit binaries to CRAN. Package developers might want to contact Uwe Ligges directly in case of questions / suggestions

You may also want to read the R FAQ and R for Windows FAQ.

Once downloaded, run the installer. Keep all default settings, except for choosing between 32 and 64 bits, depending on your machine. When you get to 'Select additional tasks' it's not really necessary to *Create a desktop shortcut*. We will be using RStudio as our interface to **R** so, as will be described shortly below, that would be our desired desktop shortcut.

For the second stage, download RStudio from

https://www.rstudio.com/products/rstudio/download/

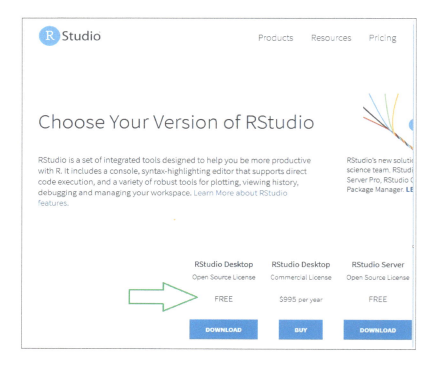

Choose the installer for your supported platform. Be aware that as pointed out in the download page:

"RStudio 1.2 requires a 64-bit operating system, and works exclusively with the 64 bit version of R. If you are on a 32 bit system or need the 32 bit version of R, you can use an older version of RStudio."

Again, most modern computers follow a 64-bit architecture, so in general that's not a problem. But if your computer is 32-bit, that's no big deal either - both the 32-bit version of **R** and the 'older' versions of RStudio work perfectly fine.

But as you probably know, the 32 vs 64 bit difference can be significant if you're going for extensive calculations; for example processing some big data sets in areas such as finance, image processing, simulation, language processing, sound, machine learning or AI algorithms. A 64-bit processor is more capable than a 32-bit processor because it can handle more data at once. 64-bit processors come in multiple-core versions which allow for an increased number of calculations per second and the maximum amount of RAM memory that is supported; which in practice is about double the number of bytes of of addressable RAM compared to the 32-bit counterparts.

These issues are magnified in the context of **R** programming because **R** processes all data precisely in RAM memory, so that, again, for large and complex datasets, this can make the difference between grabbing a cup of coffee while the computer sweats it out or taking the dog to the park for a significantly longer period of time.

In any case, execute the installer and once again you should be fine with the defaults. Just remember to keep RStudio's shortcut icon nearby in your desktop - you'll be clicking on it so many times that you'll surely wear it down and have to replace it with a new one (hopefully a newer and better version!).

You can also customize the look and appearance of RStudio to suit your liking by going to **Tools**, **Global Options**…, **Appearance**, for themes and colors, and to **Pane Layout** to change the display of the several panes in the window. I generally like to work with a dark theme (such as Twilight) for my eyesight's sake, and rearrange the panels to look something like what follows:

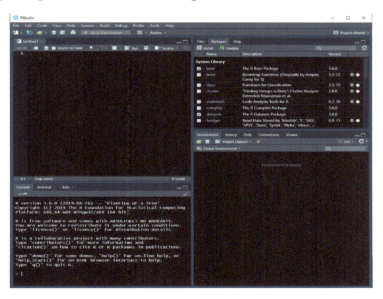

But this dark twilight theme is definitely not good for a book, so I'll change back to a **Classic RStudio** theme with a **Crimson Editor** palette. The result is shown in the following illustration:

What are all those tabs in RStudio?

Console

I'll use the pane setup I chose in the last section, but if you changed yours to whatever don't worry; the tab's contents and functionality are just the same. Also, I won't go into the details of all of those tabs, just the ones that are critical to using RStudio when you're just starting out. Having said that, most users, even advanced ones, seem to manage with just those tabs almost all of the time.

Starting with the pane that contains the **Console**, **Terminal** and **Jobs** tabs, the **Terminal** is just that - a system terminal where you can type *dir*, for example, and get a listing of the files in your current working directory (we will come back to this directory issue soon). **Jobs** was introduced in RStudio 1.2 and implements new features that can keep you going forward in your project while **R** is busy running code in the background - no need to worry about these two relatively advanced features or expressions such as '*running code in the background*' for now.

The **Console** tab is really the star of this group and is the place where you ´ll be spending a lot of time learning and working with **R**. Here's where you carry on your interactive conversations with **R**: 'Please add 1 and 1', 'What is the square root of 2?', 'Can you get the current working directory for me? I forgot where I am and I need to fetch some data', 'Print "Hello, world!" ', 'Stop running this calculation - it's still going, there's got to be a better way'.

We will do a lot of this direct interacting with **R** starting next chapter, but let's do a little something right now (just type in the inputs at the prompt (>) and press *Return* or *Enter* to get the output):

```
> 1+1
[1] 2

> print("Hello, world!")
[1] "Hello, world!"

> sqrt(8)
```

```
[1] 2.828427
> options(digits=10)
> sqrt(8)
[1] 2.828427125
> sqrt(-8)    # Maybe it doesn't work
[1] NaN
Warning message:
In sqrt(-8) : NaNs produced
```

As you can see, after you type in the third letter RStudio offers to auto-complete your commands.[1] When given a list of choices just use the arrow keys to single out the one you want and press *Tab* or *Enter*. The '*Maybe it doesn't work*' phrase after the # sign on the `> sqrt(-8)` line is a **comment** - you can populate all of **R**'s lines with comments after a given command, or write independent lines with these comments at will - they are very useful to annotate your thoughts, doubts and clarifications. Also, if you try something that **R** doesn't quite understand it will print out a friendly warning message; and if you want to go back to a certain line just use the arrow keys upwards or downward to change or correct something.

Finally, you can quickly clear the console should it become too crowded by going to **Edit**, **Clear console**; or just pressing *Ctrl-L*. Or, even easier, just press the broom icon at the top right of the console.

Editor

The bottom left pane contains the **Editor** tab, where instead of taking turns and talking interactively with **R** you can write a sort of letter (a *script*) that tells the software to carry out a sequence of commands or instructions. Those commands are just like the ones you would write at the console, but it isn't much fun to write them one by one when you can just write the script; which by the way you can reuse if you ever need to carry out basically the same sequence of steps.

As a matter of fact, as we will see shortly, you can write a one-line script, execute it, and get a result displayed at the console; which would be equivalent to just writing the same command directly at the console. Finally, the **editor** tab, among other things, lets you save your script for later use (see the '**Save**' icon on the top left of this pane); as well as run selected parts of your script - just select one

---

1 In case it bothers you, there appears to be no way to disable this behavior.

or several contiguous lines and click on **Run** or type *Ctrl-enter* as a keyboard shortcut for the **Run** command.

Go to the editor and type the following three lines:

```
1 sqrt(8)
2 sqrt(9)
3 sqrt(10)   # Third line
```

Line numbering is very useful - go to **Tools**, **Global Options...**, **Code**, **Display** and make sure that **Show line numbers** is checked.[2] Place the cursor on line 1 and click on **Run** or press *Ctrl-enter* to get the result on the console. As soon as you do this, the cursor moves down and you can just repeat the same procedure consecutively over and over again to your heart's content, just as if you were typing in each line at the console. But better yet, select the three lines and click on **Run** or press *Ctrl-enter* and all three lines will be executed immediately.

Please note that for the rest of this book instructions to **R** will be shown as if they were typed at the prompt (>) but many, especially long ones, or sequences of instructions, are easier to handle typing at the editor as part of a script, selecting and then running.

You can save the previous not-so-very-exciting three-line square root script by clicking on the aforementioned **Save** icon (which looks like a floppy disk out he 1980s) and choosing a name and location, being careful to save with the **.R** extension. But it's much better to keep things organized from the start by creating a folder for your **R** scripts and projects ('**R** scripts', for example, in your *Users* folder) and saving it there. This is usually even easier because when we create a new project (**File**, **New project** ...) RStudio helps create a *workspace* where we can keep a group of related files (for example scripts and data) together in one place. This time, being our first time, we don't need much more than any folder where to save the script file.

Moving around the file system is quite easy with the **File** and **Session** menus (please take a look at the sub-menus), making it possible to set the working directory; terminate, suspend or restart **R**; load, save or clear workspaces, and open recent files or projects. By default, when you exit RStudio and save the workspace, the next time you reopen it will take you to the place you were before; meaning that it will reopen scripts and make available the data you were working with. Needless to say, if you exit and reopen you will need to rerun your script in order to get the intermediate calculations you were working on when you quit.

---

2 Line numbers are for reference and do not form part of the script.

Packages,Help

In the upper right portion of my RStudio setup you can see the **Help**, **Packages** and **Files** tabs. RStudio enormously facilitates peeking into the language Help by just placing the cursor over whatever it is that you want to know about and pressing the F1 key. Go ahead and try it! Write *sqrt(8)* (what an obsession) at the console, place the cursor on *sqrt* and press F1. You will see the following:

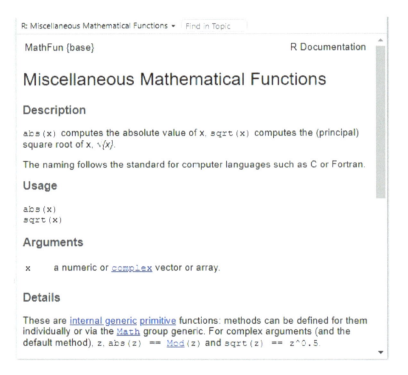

The help screen shows the object's description, arguments or parameters you must fill in (if necessary), references and -scrolling down to the very end (not shown here)- useful examples for this command. Most of the time, like 99% of the time, this help documentation solves all of our additional information needs. But if this is not enough, we can count on hundreds of Internet **R** sites and blogs, published by the worldwide **R** community, that tackle harder or less frequent problems. As we will see just below, this is also true for commands found in the thousands of additional **R** packages.

Please take a look at the contents of the **Home** icon on the **Help** tab (the little house icon on the top tool-bar), where you can also see handy forward and backward arrows that take you to previous help searches. Also look at the links on the last chapter of this book under *Help on R*.

The other (and most important) tab in this pane is the **Packages** tab. When you are just starting out in **R** and before you have downloaded additional packages, this tab just shows the core **R** packages in the System Library. In order to use any package you have to have it installed in your computer and the load it into memory. The core **R** packages are already installed, while the ones that are actually usable when you fire up RStudio are the ones that are loaded by default, marked with a check mark in the list of packages.

	Name	Description	Version	
	System Library			
✔	base	The R Base Package	3.6.0	
☐	boot	Bootstrap Functions (Originally by Angelo Canty for S)	1.3-22	⊕ ⊗
☐	class	Functions for Classification	7.3-15	⊕ ⊗
☐	cluster	"Finding Groups in Data": Cluster Analysis Extended Rousseeuw et al.	2.0.8	⊕ ⊗
☐	codetools	Code Analysis Tools for R	0.2-16	⊕ ⊗
☐	compiler	The R Compiler Package	3.6.0	
✔	datasets	The R Datasets Package	3.6.0	
☐	foreign	Read Data Stored by 'Minitab', 'S', 'SAS', 'SPSS', 'Stata', 'Systat', 'Weka', 'dBase', ...	0.8-71	⊕ ⊗
✔	graphics	The R Graphics Package	3.6.0	
✔	grDevices	The R Graphics Devices and Support for Colours and Fonts	3.6.0	
☐	grid	The Grid Graphics Package	3.6.0	
☐	KernSmooth	Functions for Kernel Smoothing Supporting Wand & Jones (1995)	2.23-15	⊕ ⊗
☐	lattice	Trellis Graphics for R	0.20-38	⊕ ⊗
☐	MASS	Support Functions and Datasets for Venables and Ripley's MASS	7.3-51.4	⊕ ⊗
☐	Matrix	Sparse and Dense Matrix Classes and Methods	1.2-17	⊕ ⊗
✔	methods	Formal Methods and Classes	3.6.0	

Among those already loaded you can see the **base** package, for example, which contains our friend the *sqrt( )* function or command.

The available version of each package is shown to the right, and if you double-click on the package's name (which is actually a link) you are taken to the **Help** tab with the information for that package, including description, demos, a list of its specific functions (commands).

Again, if the package you need is not loaded you won't be able to use its functionality. Say that you are mathematically inclined (it doesn't matter if you're not for the example) and want to construct a diagonal matrix of dimension three using the Matrix package without loading it, typing *Diagonal(3)* at the console prompt. This is what you´ll get:

```
> Diagonal(3)
Error in Diagonal(3) : could not find function "Diagonal"
```

But if you load the corresponding package, either at the console or checking the package on the package list, you'll be OK:

```
> library(Matrix)
> Diagonal(3)
3 x 3 diagonal matrix of class "ddiMatrix"
     [,1] [,2] [,3]
[1,]    1    .    .
[2,]    .    1    .
[3,]    .    .    1
```

Before moving on to the last group of tabs, a couple of warnings. When you load several packages that you're going to use for a certain task you may run into a nasty *version conflict* problem. Since packages are managed by different groups it may happen, for example, that one package's version is not updated while other packages that it depends on are; potentially generating some sort of inconsistency. Though not frequent, this situation is almost always identified and signaled by the software so that you can take corrective steps.

Also in this 'several simultaneous packages' category, you can run into *namespace* conflicts. Let's say one package implements function *bla-bla-bla*, while another package you also load into memory (authored by some other group) also contains a function named *bla-bla-bla* that does something completely different; or maybe the same thing but with different technical specs. Wow!

Although quite crude, an analogy would be if you merge Third Grade A with Third Grade B for a school activity; and it turns out that in both classes there is a person called Jean, in which case just calling 'Jean' will be totally ambiguous. In this case, **R** solves the problem by using the *double-colon operator* :: , basically distinguishing the names by calling for Third Grade A::Jane or Third Grade B::Jane. So, just to beat this to death, if a package named Matrices also contains the function Diagonal that we used above, and you loaded both this one and the above Matrix package into memory, you would then say Matrices::Diagonal(3) or Matrix::Diagonal(3) in order to solve the name clash.

RSudio signals the problem as soon as you load the second package - if you loaded Matrix into memory first. as soon as you load Matrices it would warn you like this:

```
> The following objects are masked from 'package:Matrix':

    Diagonal
```

Again, as in the case of version conflicts, this is something you need to know just in case; but it's not awfully frequent. Do not agonize over this possibility before it actually happens, and if it does you already know there's a cure.

Finally, in the top toolbar of the **Packages** tab there are two icons which help us quite a bit - Install and Update. Both are pretty much self-describing: Install does just that with packages that aren't in place already. For example, let's install *ggplot2*, a very nice graphics package for **R**. All we need to do is press on the corresponding icon:

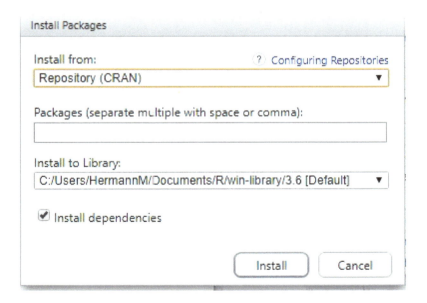

Fill in the blank where it says *Packages (separate multiple...)* with *ggplot2*; the other defaults should be just fine for now. The auto complete feature helps us along here, and then we just need to press on the *Install* button. Notice the *Install dependencies* (refers to other packages) check button, which should stay checked by default because this action is necessary in the huge majority of cases.

The download process will begin and show its progress in the console - the package you wanted to install and maybe several others will be downloaded into the default location. This particular package is heavily dependent on a bunch of others, so you may get warnings or messages along the way (*'Rtools is not installed'*, and the like) even if in principle the software should take care of the dependencies; just proceed and we'll check later on this to see if it was a fatal flaw or not.

One of the good reasons to install *ggplot2* early is not only because of its inherent usefulness but also precisely because it downloads a lot of other useful packages. You can go see for yourself that the **Packages** tab is now populated not only with the initial System Library, which now resides in the lower portion of the tab, but also with an extended User Library, which you will be extending even more as we progress in this book, and even more when you start to install the specific packages you need for your work (or hobby!).

Once installed, if you need to load *ggplot2* just load it as *library(ggplot2)* at the console prompt or check the corresponding check box in the packages listing. No need to load the dependent packages manually - the software will do this for you. If you no longer need a package (maybe to maximize available memory for other processes), just disable the corresponding check mark in the package listing.

Environment, Plots

On the lower right the **Environment** and **Plots** tabs stand out as some of the most referenced when working with RStudio.

The **Environment** tab informs us of the variables (more on this coming soon) and data that we are using and are loaded in memory in our current project. As will be seen later, custom functions can be created to complement and expand **R**'s capabilities, and all of these user-defined functions will also be shown here.

As a matter of fact **all** the entities we create in a session are listed in this **Environment** tab, which displays the basic nature and value of each one. This need for info on the beings that populate the **Environment** tab is a recurring requirement, especially when there are many of them, so **R** also gives us the possibility of further exploring the nature of these entities (or any other for that matter) with the *class* command at the console prompt. So, as an example, if you query **R** for *class(sqrt)* it will respond accordingly:

```
> class(sqrt)
[1] "function"
```

Which tells us that *sqrt* is, not surprisingly, a function. And if we explore the nature of '8', no surprises there either:

```
> class(8)
[1] "numeric"
```

This should make it clear that **R** has different types of creatures roaming around, and it is very happy to classify them according to its own peculiar taxonomy. Why does it need to do this? Well, different creatures have different sizes and characteristics, and **R** wants to keep track so it can put them in different 'cages' in memory; optimized to suit their specific nature and dimensions. As we will see later on, these 'creatures' can be anything from scalar numbers whose value is stored in a simple *variable*, to functions, to complex multidimensional *dataframes*, which can hold thousands of observations on different variables. Anything from mice to ecosystems, so to speak.

The **Plots** tab shouldn't be complicated to explain, and it is fair to point out that **R** has gained a great reputation for its publication-quality plots. Even though there are actually many graphics packages out there in the Comprehensive R Archive Network (CRAN), plots are most commonly constructed using one of the following: basic **R** functionality, lattice plots, or the previously mentioned *ggplot2*. We will have the chance to work with all of these later on. In any case, it is important to point out that any of these plots can be copied to the clipboard or saved in different formats to include in your reports, articles or books.

Finally, from the the **History** tab one can access a searchable database of all commands which have ever been entered into the console. The **Viewer** tab can be used to view local web content, and the **Connections** tab makes it possible to connect to a variety of databases from **R**. In fact, RStudio supports simultaneous database connections; but these are more advanced topics you can explore later on your own. (See for example https://db.rstudio.com/rstudio/connections/)

Basic concepts

A little bit of context

Up to this point you've been exposed to fairly prosaic things, such as how to download and install **R** and RStudio, as well as looking at the main components of R Studio's interface to **R**'s capabilities.

It's time to begin to learn some interesting stuff, and this is where pedagogical approaches differ the most. There are several to deal with teaching **R** in the literature, and of course (almost) all of them favor a gradual intro to the language and its many hallways, corners and stairways; some of them kind of steep. Here we will walk along a very practical and quick-paced path; after all, you're busy, aren't you?

The main goal is to be clear while avoiding being overly explicit. This means that you will have to observe and figure out some things by yourself. If you run into difficulties never forget the *F1* key or the ? Help system. Also, you can look things up in Google or in blogs and books listed in the final chapter under *Help on R*.

Also, it's important to insist that it is not a goal of this walk-through to be exhaustive. It will guide you to some of the most important and interesting landmarks in **R** territory so that you can get a very good feel of what **R** can do and how to do it. You will be capable of doing a lot on your own after this workout, but it is still true that practice makes perfect.

This approach also implies that you will start working with **R** and RStudio directly, and that the more 'theoretical' aspects will be covered as we go along. As with everything, this has its own pros and cons; but this methodology has been shown to be very effective at an introductory level. So, let's do it!

Fasten your seatbelts - let's go!

Go ahead and open up RStudio. We will begin by typing in a lot of calculations and functions at the console, using comments and expanding on some important concepts as the need arises. Try changing things so that you get different answers. By the way, and loosely speaking, in computing jargon a *statement* is something that carries out some action that does not yield the result of a calculation, while an *expression* does. So *print('Hello, world!')* is a statement while *sqrt(8)* is an expression. You will see examples of both in the following.

You can set the working directory (the directory where you want to place your project or script) in the Session menu, or use *setwd( )* statement with the folder name inside quotation marks.

```
> setwd("C:/Users/Myself/Documents")
> getwd()
[1] "C:/Users/Myself/Documents"
```

Let's also compute a simple *expression*:

```
> 2*3
[1] 6
```

The result of this expression is a *scalar;* an only, lonely number 6. **R** provides several types of data: Numeric (real) numbers, Integer numbers, Complex numbers, Logical values (TRUE and FALSE, in capital letters given the language's *case sensitivity*), and Character, such as the letter '*a*'. In turn, these 'atomic' types can be used to construct or process data structures of greater complexity, such as vectors, matrices or lists, as well as mixtures of types such as *dataframes*, similar to spreadsheets with columns and rows and numbers (or whatever) inside.

In any case, what if you're so impressed with *2*3* that you want to keep the result? This is simple - assign (with the *assignment operator* <-) this little creature to a small cage in memory which you can label as you wish [3], for example

---

3 Not entirely true - there are restrictions to variable names: a valid name consists of letters, numbers and the dot or underline characters and starts with a letter or the dot not followed by a

```
> mult <- 2*3    # '<' + '-' on your keyboard
> mult
[1] 6
```

Now every time you type *mult* at the prompt you will retrieve the value of that expression. Go to the **Environment** tab and look at what's listed - *mult* will be there waiting for you to carry out some action with the value it stores (try, for example, *mult*2*). You can also look at the **Environment**'s contents by typing *ls()* at the prompt.

Now is as good a time as any to save your work. You can, at any moment, save the workspace by opening **Session**, **Save Workspace As**..., which will save everything with an **.RData** extension in your current working directory, or wherever you want to save it. You can then call it a day, exit RStudio and come back next morning, reload with **Session**, **Load Workspace**... and *mult* (or whatever else) will be there for you.

Remember that if you forget the type of the creature in cage *mult,* no problem:

```
> class(mult)
[1] "numeric"
```

You can even query a class type without assigning a variable. Let's look at the type of "This is a sentence" and of the tangent function:

```
> class("This is a sentence")
[1] "character"

> class(tan)
[1] "function"
```

This last example should remind us that such *built-in functions* (**R** has hundreds of them) are very useful because we can compute, for example, the tangent of any (valid) angle just by changing the *argument* of that function (the number inside the parenthesis).

In the same vein, and going back to multiplying 2 and 3, wouldn't it be nice to get R to multiply two numbers other than those two and say something like 'The result is ' ? Clearly, we could just go to the console prompt and type in other pairs of numbers with a multiplication sign in between and get the desired result, but our intuition tells us that there must be a way to have a function that does just that, even if it's such a trivial task.

---

number. You can't use reserved words - we'll get to that later.

It turns out that there is no such built-in *f(a,b)* function in **R** (probably because the multiplication operator is enough!). But R allows us to write our own *user-defined functions*, which can enhance **R**'s possibilities enormously. We will come back briefly to this important topic again, but here's a sneak preview:

```
# Write or copy these lines in the editor, select and run

mult <- function(x,y){  # Braces { } delimit code sections
  z <- x*y
  print(paste("The result is", z))
}

> mult(8,9)       # Call the function from the console
[1] "The result is 72"
> mult(-34,26)
[1] "The result is -384"


# mult now appears in the Environment as a function
> class(mult)
[1] "function"
```

You can surely see what's going on here.

A warning - when you start writing your own functions try not to reinvent the wheel. With **R**'s thousands of packages chances are that you can use something that has already been written and tested many times, or at least something sufficiently close to what you have in mind. Take the time to Google what you want to do and also look into R blogs; this will be time well spent.

Ok, with this bit of function-related jargon in our bag let's carry on with the **R** walk-through. The next example uses a *built-in function* that generates 4 random uniform numbers. Again, the number you put inside the parenthesis is called the *argument* of the function; although there can be several arguments (*mult*).

```
> runif(4)
[1] 0.2639074 0.1269660 0.4296839 0.1941869
```

This last expression is a group of numbers and its class is numeric (run *class(runif(4))* at the console). You can of course generate as many random numbers as you please by just changing the argument of the function. Can you access just one of those numbers? Yes indeed, and this gives us a chance to look at **R**'s *indexing* capabilities; although as you will see this example is quite modest. (Spoiler - you can index, slice and subset big data structures easily in **R**, such as dataframes and databases with thousands or even millions of records).

Let's create a variable to hold our random numbers:

```
> nums <- runif(4)
> nums
[1] 0.4118128 0.6655456 0.2381011 0.8838749
```

These new numbers are different every time you run *runif( )* (they're random!). If you want a set of repeating numbers (for instance, if you want to repeat an experiment that involves randomness) you must use the *set.seed( )* built-in function (look it up! - you can type the name at the prompt or in the editor and use F1 as before, or simply type *>?set.seed( )*).

What do you think will come up at the console if you type *nums[3]* at the prompt and press *Return*? If you're thinking 0.2381011 you're right! What about *nums[2:3]* ?

```
> nums[2:3]
[1] 0.6655456 0.2381011
```

The colon sign **:** acts as a *slicing operator* – it lets you cut out pieces of data structures that are indexed, such as *nums*.

And how about two-dimensional *matrices* (arrays of *only* numbers) with rows and columns or even higher dimensional data in matrix form? Well, (in the case of a two-dimensional matrix), you use indexing in a way reminiscent of high-school algebra: double indexes, one for the row and another for the column. Same thing for higher-dimensional matrices – one index for each dimension.

```
> matdat <- matrix(c(1,2,3,11,12,13), nrow = 2, ncol = 3,
                    dimnames = list(c("row1", "row2"),
                    c("col1", "col2", "col3")))
> matdat
      col1 col2 col3
row1     1    3   12
row2     2   11   13
> matdat[1,3]
[1] 12
```

You may think of potentially higher-dimensional matrices as only abstract mathematical constructs, but they can hold very concrete information when working with real data in **R**. For instance, think of a matrix with 1000 customer names and id number, age, married status, and region on each column; for years 2000 to 2019. That would be 1001 rows high (including column names), 5 columns wide and 19 layers 'deep'.

In any case, slicing also also works here with no problem:

```
> matdat[1:2, 2:3]
     col2 col3
row1    3   12
row2   11   13
```

An empty space stands for 'all rows' or 'all columns':

```
> matdat[1, ]
col1 col2 col3
   1    3   12

> matdat[ , ]
     col1 col2 col3
row1    1    3   12
row2    2   11   13

> matdat[ ,c(1,3)]    # Look closely at this one!
     col1 col3
row1    1   12
row2    2   13
```

Several built-in functions and types were used before to construct our modest matrix - *matdat*. The **c** (*combine*) built-in function was used to specify a one-dimensional six-element vector or collection of numbers which was then transformed into a 2x3 matrix by specifying the number of rows and columns, whose names (this is not strictly necessary) were specified in *dimnames*. The number 12 in the first row and third column was retrieved using a double index [1,3] . For the sake of clarity let's look at the class of some of the components:

```
> class(matrix)
[1] "function"
> class(dimnames)
[1] "function"
> class(list)
[1] "function"
> class(c(1,2,3,11,12,13))
[1] "numeric"
> class(list(c("row1", "row2"), c("col1", "col2", "col3")))
[1] "list"
```

Should we ever want to retrieve this matrix's characteristics, **R** has many ways of doing it. You can see below that double square brackets [[ ]] are R's way of accessing elements of a *list*. Once inside the list, so to speak, you access individual elements with additional single square brackets.

```
> class(dimnames(matdat))
[1] "list

> dimnames(matdat)   # Names of rows and columns
[[1]]
[1] "row1" "row2"

[[2]]
[1] "col1" "col2" "col3"

> dimnames(matdat)[[1]][2]
[1] "row2"

> dim(matdat)         # dimensions
[1] 2 3
> length(matdat)     # how many elements
[1] 6
```

Your indexing depends on whether you're accessing elements of a vector, matrix, list, dataframe, or whatever (we will get to dataframes in a moment). If you're not sure about the type, just look at the *class( )* of whatever object you are manipulating. There's also and excellent built-in function, *str( )*, that succinctly displays the internal structure of any R object. The content displayed by this function is usually as intuitive as it is informative:

```
> str(matdat)
num [1:2, 1:3] 1 2 3 11 12 13
- attr(*, "dimnames")=List of 2
  ..$ : chr [1:2] "row1" "row2"
  ..$ : chr [1:3] "col1" "col2" "col3"
```

This says that the **str**ucture of this object, *matdat*, is a numeric container with rows 1 to 2 and columns 1 to 3, and that the values look like the sample values displayed (all of them in this case). Further, it has some non-numeric attributes (of type *chr* or 'character') which are the names of the dimensions.

Even if **R** makes it easy to construct matrices, including matrices made by hand such as *matdat*, but also matrices of ones, zeros, diagonal matrices, and so on, which are often used in computations, 'real world' matrices (or matrix-like structures such as databases, which require their own special treatment) are more likely imported from some data source such as banking records, experiments, sales records and the like. Data sources will be explored in a later chapter.

In any case, **R**'s indexing efficiency also applies to other bigger and more complex data structures such as the spreadsheet-like *dataframes*, R's most used data structure. What do they look like?

A very well-known and used example dataframe is the famous *iris* data set, which comes packed along with a lot of other 'toy' data sets in **R** (run *data( )* at the prompt) . This data set contains four features (length and width of sepals and petals) of 50 samples of three species of Iris (Iris setosa, Iris virginica and Iris versicolor). It is used frequently in Machine Learning examples to train algorithms that can learn to classify:

```
> data("iris")
> head(iris)      # Also take a look at tail()
  Sepal.Length Sepal.Width Petal.Length Petal.Width Species
1          5.1         3.5          1.4         0.2  setosa
2          4.9         3.0          1.4         0.2  setosa
3          4.7         3.2          1.3         0.2  setosa
4          4.6         3.1          1.5         0.2  setosa
5          5.0         3.6          1.4         0.2  setosa
6          5.4         3.9          1.7         0.4  setosa
```

This is a bit more complicated than *matdat* – at first it looks like a matrix but the *Species* column is a *factor*, a qualitative variable, which tend to appear repeatedly in applied work. Other non-numeric types that may crop up in columns are character or text types, and Boolean or TRUE/FALSE types.

```
> class(iris$Sepal.Length)
[1] "numeric"
> class(iris$Species)
[1] "factor"
> class(iris)
[1] "data.frame"
```

A quick test for the class reveals that this is a dataframe, but the basic indexing ideas are still easy to grasp. First, we have to learn that the Dollar sign ($) is the *selection operator* for **R** dataframes; and is used to access a column of a dataframe (also called a *variable* or a *feature*) by name. So, *iris$Sepal.Length* is the first column of this data set. Try it to convince yourself. And of course, *iris$Sepal.Length[1]* is equal to 5.1 . You can test this (which you already know is true) using the *logical operator* for equality, which is not = but == :

```
> iris$Sepal.Length[1]  == 5.1    # Two 'equals' signs
[1]  TRUE
```

With indexing, **R** allows you to (efficiently) do very powerful and cool things. Once you select a column (again, also known as a *variable* or *feature*) you can use the slicing operator at will. Some quick examples:

```
> iris$Sepal.Length[1:3]
[1] 5.1 4.9 4.7
> c(iris$Sepal.Length[1:3], iris$Sepal.Width[1:3])
[1] 5.1 4.9 4.7 3.5 3.0 3.2
# Column bind + slicing
> cbind(iris$Sepal.Length[1:3], iris$Sepal.Width[1:3])
     [,1] [,2]
[1,]  5.1  3.5
[2,]  4.9  3.0
[3,]  4.7  3.2

# Row bind + slicing
> rbind(iris$Sepal.Length[1:3], iris$Sepal.Width[1:3])
     [,1] [,2] [,3]
[1,]  5.1  4.9  4.7
[2,]  3.5  3.0  3.2

> head(iris[,1:4])
# Remember, empty means 'all', plus columns 1 to 4
  Sepal.Length Sepal.Width Petal.Length Petal.Width
1          5.1         3.5          1.4         0.2
2          4.9         3.0          1.4         0.2
3          4.7         3.2          1.3         0.2
4          4.6         3.1          1.5         0.2
5          5.0         3.6          1.4         0.2
6          5.4         3.9          1.7         0.4

> head(iris[1:6,1:4])  # Same as previous- F1 head()
  Sepal.Length Sepal.Width Petal.Length Petal.Width
1          5.1         3.5          1.4         0.2
2          4.9         3.0          1.4         0.2
3          4.7         3.2          1.3         0.2
4          4.6         3.1          1.5         0.2
5          5.0         3.6          1.4         0.2
6          5.4         3.9          1.7         0.4

> iris[1:6,] # The empty index for cols means 'all cols'
  Sepal.Length Sepal.Width Petal.Length Petal.Width Species
1          5.1         3.5          1.4         0.2  setosa
2          4.9         3.0          1.4         0.2  setosa
3          4.7         3.2          1.3         0.2  setosa
4          4.6         3.1          1.5         0.2  setosa
5          5.0         3.6          1.4         0.2  setosa
6          5.4         3.9          1.7         0.4  setosa
```

But it gets even better. You can use *relational operators* (such as greater than > , greater or equal >= , equal == , and so on) to *subset* a dataset in additional ways, extracting segments of interest beyond simple slicing. How many sepal lengths are longer than 6 inches in this sample, and which are they?

In order to answer that question, the following says 'Give me the *length* (total number of elements) in the *iris* data set, variable Sepal.Length, whose length (not R's function *length( )*, which we just used, but the physical measurement), is greater than 6 inches.

```
> length(iris$Sepal.Length[iris$Sepal.Length > 6])
[1] 61

> which(iris$Sepal.Length > 6)  # Which? - give me the
indexes
  [1]    51   52   53   55   57   59   64   66   69   72   73   74   75   76
        77
 [16]    78   87   88   92   98  101  103  104  105  106  108  109  110  111
        112
 [31]  113  116  117  118  119  121  123  124  125  126  127  128  129  130
        131
 [46]  132  133  134  135  136  137  138  140  141  142  144  145  146  147
        148
 [61]  149

> iris$Sepal.Length[51]    # A single value at index number 51
[1] 7

> idx <- c(53,55,57)
> iris$Sepal.Length[idx]  # Values at indexes 53,55 and 57
[1] 6.9 6.5 6.3
```

Often times you will need to combine conditions, such as 'Income less than (some number) *and* age greater than (some number)'. For this you will use *logical* and *relational operators*. For example, the ampersand symbol in **R** (&) is a *logical operator* that means '*and* '. The following table summarizes available logical and relational operators:

Operator	Meaning
&	Element-wise *And*
| (pipe)	Element-wise *Or*
&&	Logical *And*
|| (double pipe)	Logical *Or*
isTRUE(x)	Test whether X is TRUE
!	Negation
<	Less than
<=	Less than or equal to
>	Greater than
>=	Greater than or equal to
==	Equal to
!=	Not equal to

Using those operators, you can implement everything from very simple tests to conditions of greater complexity and interest:

```
> 3 == 4
[1] FALSE
> 'abc' != 'ABC'    # R is case-sensitive
[1] TRUE

> which(iris$Sepal.Length > 6 & iris$Sepal.Width > 3.5)
[1] 110 118 132

# Watch out!
> which(iris$Sepal.Length > 6 && iris$Sepal.Width > 3.5)
integer(0)
```

Lots more efficient than spreadsheet pivot tables, with all respect! You can surely imagine 'real life' applications easily, even dealing with millions of observations: Which clients are behind in their payments whose ages are between 34 and 45? Which patients have been diagnosed with a heart ailment whose blood pressure exceeds certain values, are aged over 50 and live in a specific region? You get it!

This last potential search example is interesting because it includes a variable -*region*- that is not a quantitative but rather a *qualitative* variable or *factor,* which we have mentioned before. It's important to go back a little and add to what we've already said that these variables appear in dataframes as text but in practice are coded numerically for processing.[4] An example is the *Species* variable in our iris dataframe:

```
> class(iris$Species)
[1] "factor"
> levels(iris$Species)
[1] "setosa"     "versicolor" "virginica"
> str(iris$Species)  # Numerically coded as 1, 2, 3
 Factor w/ 3 levels "setosa","versicolor",..: 1 1 1 1 1 1 ...
```

These creatures join the family of **R** types in their own right, and **R** has many functions for dealing with them. For example, it obviously doesn't make any sense to compute the mean of the variable *Species,* but you can make a *table( )* (built-in function) to count the number of occurrences of each in the sample:

---

4   Those of you familiar with Statistics know that factors can be *ordered* ('Cold', 'Pleasant', 'Warm', 'Hot') or *unordered.* ('Female', 'Male'). Also, kno w that by default, *data.frame( )* converts character vectors into factors. If this is not wanted, pass the argument *stringsAsFactors* = *FALSE* to that *function.*

```
> table(iris$Species)

    setosa versicolor  virginica
        50          50         50
```

Even more interesting, how about the distribution of petal width according to species?

```
> iris_table <-  table(iris$Species, iris$Petal.Width)

> iris_table

            0.1 0.2  0.3 0.4 0.5 0.6 1  1.1 1.2 1.3 1.4 1.5 1.6
  setosa      5  29    7   7   1   1 0    0   0   0   0   0   0
  versicolor  0   0    0   0   0   0 7    3   5  13   7  10   3
  virginica   0   0    0   0   0   0 0    0   0   0   1   2   1

            1.7 1.8 1.9 2  2.1 2.2 2.3 2.4 2.5
  setosa      0   0   0 0    0   0   0   0   0
  versicolor  1   1   0 0    0   0   0   0   0
  virginica   1  11   5 6    6   3   8   3   3
```

We just learned that most (29) of the *setosa* specimens have a petal width of just 0.2 inches!

Here's a table with a predefined condition:

```
> table(iris$Sepal.Length > 5.0)

FALSE   TRUE
   32    118
```

Calculate frequencies:

```
> margin.table(iris_table, 1) # Species  - sum over rows

    setosa versicolor  virginica
        50         50         50
```

```
# Petal width frequencies (summed over columns)

> margin.table(iris_table, 2)   # Only first row shown

0.1 0.2 0.3 0.4 0.5 0.6  1 1.1 1.2 1.3 1.4 1.5 1.6 1.7 1.8
  5  29   7   7   1   1  7   3   5  13   8  12   4   2  12
```

And the corresponding proportions:

```
# Row percentages (second parameter = 1)
> prop.table(iris_table, 1)    # Partial display

               0.1  0.2  0.3  0.4  0.5  0.6    1  1.1  1.2  1.3
    setosa    0.10 0.58 0.14 0.14 0.02 0.02 0.00 0.00 0.00 0.00
    versicolor 0.00 0.00 0.00 0.00 0.00 0.00 0.14 0.06 0.10 0.26
    virginica 0.00 0.00 0.00 0.00 0.00 0.00 0.00 0.00 0.00 0.00

# column percentages (second parameter = 2)
> prop.table(ptlwidth_table, 2) # Partial display

                     0.1        0.2        0.3        0.4
    setosa     1.00000000 1.00000000 1.00000000 1.00000000
    versicolor 0.00000000 0.00000000 0.00000000 0.00000000
    virginica  0.00000000 0.00000000 0.00000000 0.00000000
```

This is an outstanding feature in R - one can easily map all types of operations over data structures. Technically, this is related to **R**'s vectorization capacities, as well as the fact that it is mostly a *functional programming language*, for which *mappings* are very natural.

As additional examples, let's take some simple vectors and play around with them. The first is a vector of weights in Kilos, which is easily transformed into pounds multiplying by a scalar. The operation is *vectorized* so it is carried out over each and every one of the components:

```
> weightsKg  <-  c(45,66,78,84,56)
> weightsLbs <- 2.2 * weightsKg
> weightsLbs
[1]  99.0 145.2 171.6 184.8 123.2
```

It's just as easy to create a range or sequence of numbers and apply operations on all the values:

```
> range1 <- 1:15  # range returns a vector containing the
minimum and maximum

> range1
[1]  1  2  3  4  5  6  7  8  9 10 11 12 13 14 15

> sqrt(range1)   # OK, I promise no more square roots!
[1] 1.000000 1.414214 1.732051 2.000000 2.236068 2.449490
[7] 2.645751 2.828427 3.000000 3.162278 3.316625 3.464102
[13] 3.605551 3.741657 3.872983
```

```
# same as 1:15, but as shown below seq is more flexible.

> seq(15)
 [1]  1  2  3  4  5  6  7  8  9 10 11 12 13 14 15

> seq(0, 1, length.out = 11)  # Specify how many elements
 [1] 0.0 0.1 0.2 0.3 0.4 0.5 0.6 0.7 0.8 0.9 1.0

> seq(1,9,by = 2)      # Increment by two
 [1] 1 3 5 7 9

> seq(1.575, 3.125, by = 0.35)
 [1] 1.575 1.925 2.275 2.625 2.975
```

Some heavily-used vectorized and mapped **R** functions are very handy when dealing with larger data sets, especially dataframes. Going back to the *iris* dataset, see how easy it is to apply several functions (mean, median,...) at once, all contained in turn in the function *summary( )*:

```
> summary(iris)
  Sepal.Length    Sepal.Width     Petal.Length    Petal.Width          Species
 Min.   :4.300   Min.   :2.000   Min.   :1.000   Min.   :0.100   setosa    :
50
 1st Qu.:5.100   1st Qu.:2.800   1st Qu.:1.600   1st Qu.:0.300
versicolor:50
 Median :5.800   Median :3.000   Median :4.350   Median :1.300   virginica :
50
 Mean   :5.843   Mean   :3.057   Mean   :3.758   Mean   :1.199
 3rd Qu.:6.400   3rd Qu.:3.300   3rd Qu.:5.100   3rd Qu.:1.800
 Max.   :7.900   Max.   :4.400   Max.   :6.900   Max.   :2.500
```

There is also a large family of *apply* functions that apply functions (yes!) to datasets so that we may obtain additional information from them. For instance,

```
# The second argument is '1' for rows or '2' for columns

> apply(iris[,1:4], 2, mean)
Sepal.Length  Sepal.Width Petal.Length  Petal.Width
    5.843333     3.057333     3.758000     1.199333
```

You can explore other members of the *apply* family - *apply()*, *lapply( )*, *sapply( )*, *tapply( )* and *mapply( )*. All of these functions are alternatives to *loops* (repetitive actions), which we will explore later.

The *aggregate( )* function is incredibly useful when applying functions to dataframes and its general syntax is *aggregate(x, by, FUN, ..., simplify = TRUE)*. Here, the data object is *x*, *by* specifies the field by which we want to aggregate and *FUN* the function we want to apply.

```
> aggregate(iris$Sepal.Length, by = list(iris$Petal.Length,
  iris$Species), mean)  # Only first 12 rows displayed here
    Group.1    Group.2      x
1       1.0     setosa 4.600000
2       1.1     setosa 4.300000
3       1.2     setosa 5.400000
4       1.3     setosa 4.842857
5       1.4     setosa 4.915385
6       1.5     setosa 5.146154
7       1.6     setosa 4.914286
8       1.7     setosa 5.400000
9       1.9     setosa 4.950000
10      3.0 versicolor 5.100000
11      3.3 versicolor 4.950000
12      3.5 versicolor 5.350000
```

So, for example, the average sepal length for the *setosa* variety of petal length 1.6 is 4.914286 inches. And, looking at the previous result, you can figure out the next line. Remember to place the cursor over unknown terms and press F1 if you want more information.

```
> sort(unique(iris$Petal.Length)) # Only first 12 values
shown
[1] 1.0 1.1 1.2 1.3 1.4 1.5 1.6 1.7 1.9 3.0 3.3 3.5
```

Very efficient indeed! Let's do a couple more so you get the hang of it. The syntax is slightly different than the previous example.

```
> aggregate(Sepal.Length ~ Species, iris, mean)
# No need for $ sign, specifies data source (iris)
     Species Sepal.Length
1     setosa        5.006
2 versicolor        5.936
3  virginica        6.588

> aggregate(Sepal.Length ~ Petal.Length + Species, iris,
mean)
# Same as previous page, different syntax (only first 12
rows)
  Petal.Length    Species Sepal.Length
1          1.0     setosa     4.600000
2          1.1     setosa     4.300000
3          1.2     setosa     5.400000
4          1.3     setosa     4.842857
5          1.4     setosa     4.915385
6          1.5     setosa     5.146154
7          1.6     setosa     4.914286
8          1.7     setosa     5.400000
9          1.9     setosa     4.950000
```

```
10              3.0 versicolor      5.100000
11              3.3 versicolor      4.950000
12              3.5 versicolor      5.350000
> aggregate(cbind( Sepal.Length, Sepal.Width) ~ Species,
              iris, mean)
     Species Sepal.Length Sepal.Width
1      setosa        5.006       3.428
2  versicolor        5.936       2.770
3   virginica        5.588       2.974
```

This last example makes use of the previously mentioned *cbind( )* function to bind two columns of the dataframe in order to carry out the aggregation. You may recall that there is a twin *rbind( )* function for rows.

It's important to point out that the specialized *data.table* package does this sort of thing and much more: subset rows, select and carry out calculations on columns, and perform aggregations like the one we've been doing.[5] With big and complex datasets it's what you should probably use instead of trying to squeeze too much out of *aggregate( )*. In particular, check out the *subset( )* function, included in both the *data.table* and *base* packages.

Finally, let's imagine that at this point we have reached an elevated mountain overlook in our travels through **R**land. Let's stop for while, catch our breath, look around and think back at what's happened.

Well, in summary, we started out with scalars, variables and simple calculations, stepped quickly over functions and continued to more complex data structures, all the way from vectors and matrices to dataframes. Built-in functions such as *class( )* and *str( )* helped us understand the nature and contents of these data structures.

Along the way, we saw factors, tables, logical and relational operators; all of which extend our capacity to build interesting filters and conditions. But perhaps the most important thing to remember up to now from this relatively rapid sightseeing expedition is that **R** has a set of mechanisms - indexing, slicing, sub-setting, vectorization and mapping - that make it incredibly efficient to explore, summarize, modify and extract information from all of those data structures.

You can actually do a lot with you've learned so far, but in the following chapters we will focus briefly on four topics that will round off your general knowledge of the **R** landscape: getting data, constructing graphics, handling time series and using control structures in your programs.

---

5 Another very useful and utilized package for this sort of task and many other data manipulation problems is *dplyr*.

Getting data

In previous chapters we utilized made-up or imported data from **R**'s stock of practice datasets. In real life, however, you'll be using data collected by your organization, or from some other national or international one, a web site, a database or in real time from an actual running process such as the Stock Exchange, weather stations or the Internet of Things. In all cases, although we won't go through all of them, R is well-suited to handle large and complex amounts of data.

In the simplest of cases you'll want to load data from a local source such as a spreadsheet or CSV file on your hard disk; or from one of those same types of files on the Web. Reading CSV files is one of the most common ways to get data into memory, so let's begin with that. Really, what you need to do is just what your common sense would tell you to do - get the location of the file, download it to a local dataframe, check to see if everything is OK and (possibly) save it to your workspace.

The most used function for this task is called *read.table( )*,[6] which results in an **R** dataframe, and is actually part of a family of functions that achieve the same purpose but with slightly different levels of specialization.

```
read.table(file, header = FALSE, sep = "", quote = "\"'",
           etc.)
read.csv(file, header = TRUE, sep = ",", quote = "\"",
         dec = ".", etc.)
read.csv2(file, header = TRUE, sep = ";", quote = "\"",
          dec = ",", etc.)
read.delim(file, header = TRUE, sep = "\t", quote = "\"",
           dec = ".", etc.)
read.delim2(file, header = TRUE, sep = "\t", quote = "\"",
            dec = ",", etc.)
```

---

6 As you advance in your knowledge of R and its data handling capabilities you will meet more specific functions such as *unzip( )* and specialized packages such as *readxl* for reading Excel files, not to mention all sorts of possible connections with databases.

You can immediately see in the corresponding documentation that these functions have a taste for eating up large amounts of parameters in order to adjust to a variety of possible situations, although for the most part the first three are the most important; the rest can usually be left at their default values. The aforementioned *read.table( )* function is pretty general, and as explained in the corresponding **Help** documentation

"read.csv and read.csv2 are identical to read.table except for the defaults. They are intended for reading 'comma separated value' files ('.csv') or (read.csv2) the variant used in countries that use a comma as decimal point and a semicolon as field separator. Similarly, read.delim and read.delim2 are for reading delimited files, defaulting to the TAB character for the delimiter."

So, let's get going: in the following a CSV file with housing characteristics is downloaded, assigned to an **R** file and the *head( )* is then shown (only part of it displayed here):

```
> fileURL <- "https://d396qusza40orc.cloudfront.net/getdata
          %2Fdata%2Fss06hid.csv"

> download.file(fileURL, destfile =
              "C:/Users/Myself/Downloads/housing.csv")

  trying URL 'https://d396qusza40orc.cloudfront.net/getdata
          %2Fdata%2Fss06hid.csv'

  Content type 'text/csv' length 4246554 bytes (4.0 MB)
  downloaded 4.0 MB

  # Remember to set working directory
> housing <- read.csv("C:/Users/Myself/Downloads/
                    housing.csv")

> head(housing)    # Only part of head() shown here
   RT SERIALNO DIVISION PUMA REGION ST  ADJUST WGTP NP TYPE
1  H       186        8  700      4 16 1015675   89  4    1
2  H       306        8  700      4 16 1015675  310  1    1
3  H       395        8  100      4 16 1015675  106  2    1
4  H       506        8  700      4 16 1015675  240  4    1
5  H       835        8  800      4 16 1015675  118  4    1

> str(housing)
'data.frame':        6496 obs. of  188 variables:
 $ RT      : Factor w/ 1 level "H": 1 1 1 1 1 1 1 1 1 1 ...
 $ SERIALNO: int  186 306 395 506 835 989 1861 2120 2278 2428
 $ DIVISION: int  8 8 8 8 8 8 8 8 8 8 ...
 $ PUMA    : int  700 700 100 700 800 700 700 200 400 500 ...
```

```
$ REGION  : int  4 4 4 4 4 4 4 4 4 4 ...
$ ST      : int  16 16 16 16 16 16 16 16 16 16 ...
$ ADJUST  : int  1015675 1015675 1015675 1015675 1015675
$ WGTP    : int  89 310 106 240 118 115 0 35 47 51 ...
$ NP      : int  4 1 2 4 4 4 1 2 2 ...
$ TYPE    : int  1 1 1 1 1 1 2 1 1 1 ...
$ ACR     : int  1 NA 1 1 2 1 NA 1 1 1 ...
$ AGS     : int  NA NA NA NA 1 NA NA NA NA NA ...
```

This is a relatively complex dataframe (6496 obs. of 188 variables, including factors and missing values). The advantages of **R**'s functions are truly critical in these situation vis-à-vis, for example, what you would have available in a spreadsheet; not to mention the resources required at a larger scale, say, a Big Data application.

But, as always, we have got to be very careful when handling the data; making sure that the data are usable and tidy before working with them. For example, if we call the summary function on this dataframe we get the following, which ignores NAs by default so that the statistics differ in number of cases depending on the presence or absence of NAs:

```
> summary(housing)   # Partial display
  RT         SERIALNO        DIVISION        PUMA          REGION
 H:6496   Min.   :    186   Min.   :8   Min.   :100.0   Min.   :4
          1st Qu.: 346442   1st Qu.:8   1st Qu.:300.0   1st Qu.:4
          Median : 686950   Median :8   Median :500.0   Median :4
          Mean   : 684134   Mean   :8   Mean   :486.2   Mean   :4
          3rd Qu.:1024785   3rd Qu.:8   3rd Qu.:700.0   3rd Qu.:4
```

From the information given by the *str( )* function above, we have to proceed carefully with variables such as RT (a *factor* - see the documentation for *as.factor( )*); as well as variables like ACR, which show NAs (missing values) early on in *str( )* for the second and seventh observations, but seem to have no problem presenting all the usual statistics in *summary( )*. Again, this is because *summary( )* ignores NAs by default, but you have to make sure that this is what you want: maybe you want to interpolate or otherwise estimate those missing values; maybe missing values for this variable represent 88% of all observations and it's just not worth it.

And what if the dataframe has many thousands or even millions of records (rows) and columns and we can't easily see those potential problems from what *str( )* succinctly shows?

No problem - **R**'s built in functions, such as *is.na( )* or *complete.cases( )* come to the rescue. Additionally, many of **R**'s data processing built-in functions include as an argument or parameter an option to include or exclude (remove, *rm*) missing values so you can choose whatever is best suited for a particular task.

For example, for some given vector *x1* you can say *mean(x1, na.rm = TRUE)*. As mentioned, this *na.rm* is an option in many function arguments throughout **R** - just be careful when to set it to TRUE or take some other action, such as the possibility raised before of interpolating those missing values.

```
> x1 <- c(1,2,NA,3, 56)
> mean(x1)
[1] NA
> mean(x1, na.rm = TRUE)
[1] 15.5

# Column (variable) means
> colMeans(housing[, 2:5], na.rm = TRUE)
    SERIALNO     DIVISION         PUMA       REGION
 684133.6813       8.0000     486.2223       4.0000
```

On the other hand, the *is.na( )* function yields TRUE or FALSE (which in R are coded as 1 or 0) so that you can detect these missing values and count how many there are. You have to set the non-numerical values to *NA* for the *is.na( )* function to work properly. For instance,

```
> is.na(c(1, NA))
[1] FALSE  TRUE
> is.na(c(1, 2, 3, NA))
[1] FALSE FALSE FALSE  TRUE
> is.na(c(1, 2.3456, 3, 'a', NA))
[1] FALSE FALSE FALSE FALSE  TRUE
> is.na(c(1, 2.3456, 3, NA, NA))
[1] FALSE FALSE FALSE  TRUE  TRUE
# NA stands for missing values, "NA" is text
> is.na( c("a", "B", NA, "NA"))
[1] FALSE FALSE  TRUE FALSE
> is.na( c("a", "B", NA, "NA", NaN,"NaN"))
[1] FALSE FALSE  TRUE FALSE FALSE FALSE
# Built-in sum() function, the base package also has mean,
# median, sd, etc.
> sum(is.na(c(1,2.3456,3,NA, NA)))
[1] 2
```

Finally, the *complete.cases( )* function returns a logical vector (full of TRUE and FALSE values, one for each entry) indicating which cases are complete.

```
> sum(complete.cases(housing$RT))   # All cases are complete
[1] 6496
```

```
> sum(complete.cases(housing$AGS)) # Only 21.9% complete
[1] 1422
```

You can then use this logical vector to subset (index) the valid part of your data to calculate some quantity of interest:

```
# Coincides with summary()
> mean(housing$AGS[complete.cases(housing$AGS)])
[1] 1.584388
> mean(housing$AGS, na.rm = TRUE)
[1] 1.584388
```

See also NaN and anyNA. The functions *na.omit( )* and *na.exclude( )* return objects with observations removed if they contain any missing values.

This *data munging*, sometimes called *data wrangling*, *data cleaning* or *data tidying* process is of the utmost importance and is of itself an art and a science. Remember - garbage in, garbage out! Be sure to expand your knowledge of R's capabilities in this area to use them fully to your advantage.

There are other of ways of acquiring data with **R** that we should mention before moving on to graphics (although we'll be creating a couple of them in what follows as a warm-up). For example, one can easily hook up to economic-financial data using packages like *quantmod* and *jsonlite* and extract information from the Web in no time. By the way, 'AAPL' is the symbol for Apple Inc., and your common sense and general knowledge will guide you through the next series of commands, even if you are not a quant.

```
> install.packages("quantmod")
> install.packages("jsonlite")
> library(quantmod)
> library(jsonlite)
> yahooQuote.EOD
[[1]]
[1] "ohgllv"

[[2]]
[1] "Open"    "High"    "Low"     "Close"   "Volume"

attr(,"class")
[1] "quoteFormat"

> aapl <- getQuote("AAPL")
> aapl  # Partial display
            Trade Time    Last    Change % Change    Open
AAPL 2019-07-01 16:00:01 201.55 3.630005 1.834077 203.17
```

```
> aapl["Volume"]    # Or whatever
        Volume
AAPL 24891887

# Japan/US exchange rate and platinum spot price

> setSymbolLookup(DEXJPUS='FRED')
# Platinum spot
> setSymbolLookup(XPTUSD=list(name="XPT/USD",src="oanda"))
> setwd("F:/R Walkthrough")   # Adjust
> saveSymbolLookup(file="lookup.rda")
# For a later session load as:
> loadSymbolLookup(file="lookup.rda")

> getSymbols(c("DEXJPUS","XPTUSD"))
[1] "DEXJPUS" "XPTUSD"
> # Plot
> plot(DEXJPUS)    # Be sure to go to the Plots pane.
> getSymbols("AAPL")
> barChart(AAPL)
> addMACD()       # Moving Average Convergence Divergence
> addBBands()   # Bollinger bands
```

If you followed along and actually got the data and plotted it, you'll probably agree that this is pretty cool. In the next chapter we will be looking further into **R**'s graphics capabilities, which as you will see are highly developed.

Graphics

R's graphics capabilities have earned it a well-deserved reputation in the field of data visualization. We have gone through a couple of examples before, but if you want to get a general feel for what's available you can run *demo('graphics')* at the prompt, or look at a wide variety of examples at sites such as *The R Graph Gallery* (https://www.r-graph-gallery.com/)

The **R** graphics system is really composed of several packages, some very near to **R**'s core, others more towards the periphery. Those nearest the core and widely used are the graphics routines associated with the *base* package, the *lattice* plots package and Hadley Wickam's *ggplot2*. Although there are many other packages near to R's core, these are again the most used; and you can basically do whatever you need to do with these three packages. In any case, make sure to check out the *CRAN Task View: Graphic Displays & Dynamic Graphics & Graphic Devices & Visualization*.

Other 'peripheral' packages such as *highcharter, Leaflet, Plotly, dygraphs* and others are basically **R** wrappers or interfaces to other libraries written in other languages. We won't be looking into these packages here but please take some time out to explore these other alternatives.

The core *base* graphics capabilities revolve around the *plot( )* function, its parameters and additional or complementary commands; which serve to change or add components to the final graphic. A very simple base line plot can be specified as follows:

```
> plot(sin, -pi, 2*pi)
```

Make sure to use the **Zoom** option if you want to see the graphic as it would be printed, and to explore the **Export** tab and learn about the clipboard and format options for your reports.

This simple plot can be improved by adding parameter options to the basic *plot( )* command. Among the most useful ones are *color* and *title (main title)*:

```
> plot(sin,-pi,2*pi,col="blue", main="The sine function")
# Plot it!
```

These line plots are used very frequently, but there are many other options. Box plots, for example, are very informative; and *base* plotting again makes it easy to implement them.[7] The interpretation of these results is up to you...

```
> boxplot(Sepal.Length ~ Petal.Length, data = iris, col =
           "orange", main = "Dispersion of sepal length
           conditional on petal length", xlab = "Petal
           Length",ylab = "Sepal Length")
```

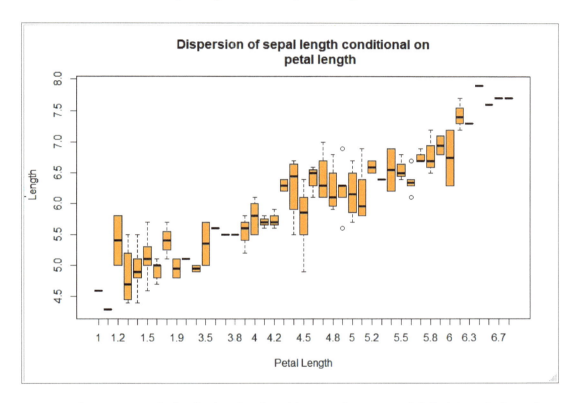

If you are statistically inclined and have a *linear model* (*lm*) in mind, such as a regression of Sepal.Length on Sepal.Width (no formal hypothesis, just for fun), the *plot( )* function produces a series of useful graphics (residuals vs fitted, Normal Q-Q, scale location, residuals vs leverage) by just plotting the *lm* result:

```
# Dependent variable and regressors separated in formula by a
  squiggle '~'
> linmod <- lm(Sepal.Length ~ Sepal.Width, data = iris)
> plot(linmod)  # Only one of four plots shown here
```

7 Remember that instructions to **R** are shown as if they were typed at the prompt (>) but many, especially these long ones, or sequences of instructions, are easier to handle typing at the editor as part of a script, selecting and then running.

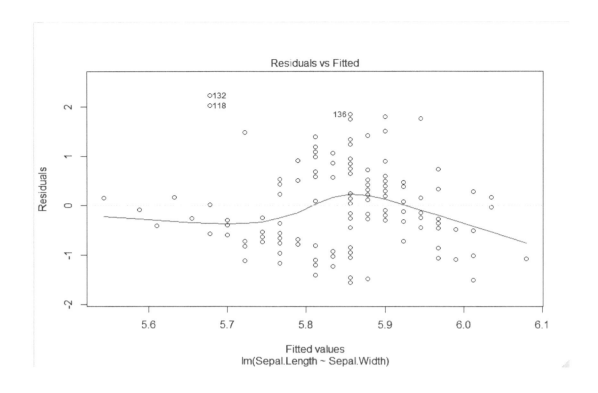

An *array of graphics* can be implemented by adjusting the plot device's parameters and margins. For example, two histograms related to our dear *iris* dataset (plot them, and for practice you may of course improve the appearance):

```
# The par() function can be used to adjust margins and
   layout. Also, see documentation for the subset() function
> par(mfrow = c(2, 1), mar = c(4, 4, 2, 1))
> hist(subset(iris, Species == "setosa")$Sepal.Length, col =
      "gray80")
> hist(subset(iris, Species == "virginica")$Sepal.Length, col
      = "lightblue")
```

As you can see from these examples, *base* plotting is carried out in two phase: initialize and annotate. You start with one of the plotting functions and then add annotations such as lines, points, axis or text.

The *lattice* plotting system written by Deepayan Sarkar tends to emphasize visualization of multivariate relationships and offers support for Trellis graphics (graphs that show a variable or related variables -for example x and y- conditioned on one or more other factors), and is independent from the base graphics we've seen so far. In this case the *grid* package is the basis upon which the graphing system is initialized, and the *lattice* package builds on top of that grid.

In contrast to the two phases in *base* plotting *lattice* graphics employs a single function call (which can be kind of complicated and somewhat inflexible), but at the same time automatically sets some important parameters and thus can make life easier in some respects.

Lattice functions include -among others- barcharts, scatterplots, contour plots, box and whiskers plots, histograms, and violin plots. These functions are specified by means of a *formula* that singles out the interrelated variables to display, separated by a ~ (squiggle) symbol, and then separated by a | (pipe symbol) from the the conditioning factors; such as g1, g2, and so on.

The formula is thus of the form y ~ x | g1 * g2 * ... (or y ~ x | g1 + g2 + ...)[8] producing plots of y (on the y-axis) versus x (on the x-axis) conditional on g1, g2, ...

In other words, create a plot for every unique value of **g** or combination of factors. Here x and y are the *primary variables*, and g1, g2, ... are the *conditioning variables*. A *grouping variable* may also be specified.

Perhaps the best way to see this is with a series of scatterplot examples; each one adding further specs. The resulting graphic is displayed on the following page.

```
# Install, if you haven't done so already

> install.packages("lattice")

> Library("lattice")              # Load

> xyplot(Sepal.Length ~ Petal.Length, data = iris)

> xyplot(Sepal.Length ~ Petal.Length, group = Species, data =
        iris, auto.key = TRUE)

> xyplot(Sepal.Length ~ Petal.Length | Species, group =
        Species, data = iris, type = c("p", "smooth"),
        scales = "free")
```

---

8 g1*g2 means 'for every combination of factors g1 and g2'.

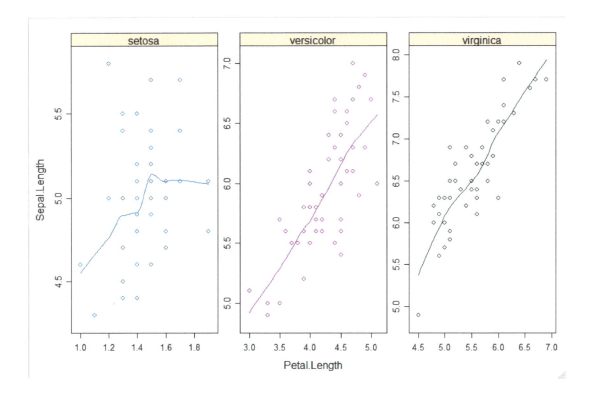

This is of course a very short intro to lattice graphics, and it is important to point out that many enhancements to the Lattice system are available in the *latticeExtra* package.

Finally, in this group, the *ggplot2* package written by Hadley Wickham implements the *grammar of graphics* (gg) paradigm of Leland Wilkinson in **R;** also building on the above mentioned grid graphics infrastructure. This approach constructs graphics from three fundamental components: *data* (the dataframe), *aesthetics* and *geometry*. Aesthetics indicates the variables and controls modifiers such as color, size and shape; while geometry defines the type of graphics.

There are two modalities and corresponding functions in *ggplot2*: *qplot( )* and *ggplot( )*. The former specifies a quick plot; which is used for, well, quick and simple plots, and is analogous to the base *plot( )* function. The *ggplot( )* function is more comprehensive and lets you build beautiful, informative plots in a layer by layer style of work. These layers, as we will explore below, include components such as *geoms*, which are geometric objects like points or lines; *facets* or conditional plots; *stats* or statistical transformations such as smoothing, and a *coordinate system* in which data are displayed. Plot the following examples and see those layers in action.

```
> install.packages('ggplot2')
> library(ggplot2)

> qplot(Sepal.Length. Petal.Width, data = iris, color =
        Species, shape = Species)
```

Nice and quick, wasn't it? You can see some sort of relation, maybe linear, between those two variables in the previous graph. So let's add a smooth mean line with a 95% confidence interval (a *geom*) using linear regression (*lm*). This is just a way to calculate a line that lies closest to all the points in each group and draw bands of confidence that depend on the dispersion within each of those groups.

```
> qplot(Sepal.Length. Petal.Width, data = iris, color =
        Species, shape = Species, geom = c("point","smooth"),
        method="lm")
```

Facets are similar to panels in *lattice* and their job is also to split data by conditioning on factor variables. Here, the expression *facets = . ~ columns* creates 1 x number of columns subplots:

```
> qplot(Sepal.Length. Petal.Width, data = iris, facets = . ~
        Species, color = Species, shape = Species)
```

The *ggplot( )* function builds up by layers and has the general form *gr <- ggplot(data, aes(var1, var2))*, where *aes* specifies the aesthetics component or components. We must first initialize the graphics object *gr*, or whatever you want to call it, and then add the layers using the ' + ' symbol.

```
gr <- ggplot( data = iris) + geom_density( aes( x =
            Sepal.Width), fill = "grey80")
```

If you run *str(gr)* after doing this **R** will show you the intricate inner structure of this graphic, and you will also have a greater understanding about the different components and layers.

And just to insist on the layers methodology, let's reconstruct one of the previous quick plots but go a little further adding new layers:

```
> gr <- ggplot( iris, aes( x = Sepal.Length, y =
            Petal.Width))
# Nothing!
> gr + geom_point( aes( color = Species))
> gr + geom_point( aes( color = Species)) + facet_wrap( ~
            Species)
# There you have it!
```

It would be absolutely unforgivable to end this very short tour of *ggplot2* without mentioning one of its distinctive and most versatile features: *themes*. While it can be forbidding to implement one of these from scratch, there are packages such as *ggthemes*, which re-create several styles of graphs. The next two plots – two different themes - are shown below for comparison

```
> Install(ggthemes)
> library(ggthemes)
> g2 <- ggplot( iris, aes( x = Petal.Width, y =
            Sepal.Length)) + geom_point( aes( color =
            Species))
> g2 + theme_gray() + scale_color_canva()
> g2 + theme_clean() + scale_colour_few()
```

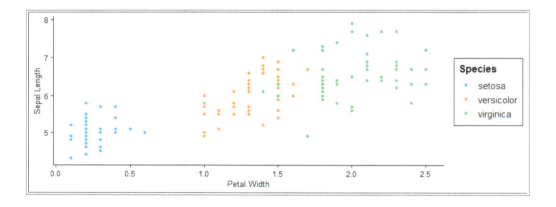

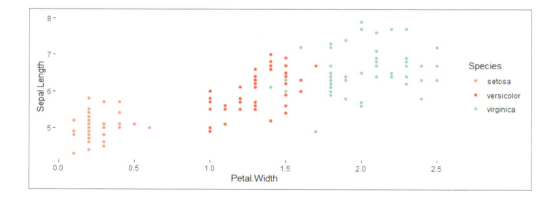

Be aware that there are lots of themes to choose from:

- Theme Base
- Theme Calc
- Clean ggplot theme
- ggplot color theme based on the Economist
- ggplot color theme based on the Economist
- ggplot theme based on old Excel plots
- ggplot theme similar to current Excel plot defaults
- Theme based on Few's "Practical Rules for Using Color in Charts"
- Theme inspired by fivethirtyeight.com plots
- Foundation Theme
- Theme with Google Docs Chart defaults
- Highcharts Theme
- Inverse gray theme
- Clean theme for maps
- ggplot color themes based on the Solarized palette
- ggplot color themes based on the Solarized palette
- Theme with nothing other than a background color
- Themes based on Stata graph schemes
- Tufte Maximal Data, Minimal Ink Theme
- Wall Street Journal theme

Datetimes and Time Series

A time series is a sequence of measurements taken (usually) at successive equally-spaced time intervals, such as seconds, days, months or years. Weather data, data generated by devices hooked onto the Internet of Things, economic and financial data and keeping track of your weight on a weekly basis are all examples of time series.

A distinguishing feature of these measurements is that they are inextricably tied to a time stamp or index. These are not regular 1,2,3... indexes, or customer ids, or quantities associated with specific regions - time series analysis and visualization requires dealing with time and time-keeping; which has a lot of twists and turns.

This time-keeping activity is as old as Humanity, and just about every civilization has come up with its own solutions. Devices such as sundials, water clocks, candles, hourglasses, mechanical devices and atomic clocks have been used as instruments of measurement, but the really interesting thing about these devices is that they were never socially neutral: they belong to systems of measurement tied to specific economic contexts, astronomical knowledge and religious practices. However, Europe's Renaissance and Industrial Revolution propelled the spread of commercial and financial activities that assisted the globalization of the Gregorian Calendar, western time standards and the use of mechanical clocks to almost every corner of the globe. Most widely-used modern software to this day uses this calendar and time standards, and **R** is no exception.

And yet, even with an almost universal calendar and time standards system, handling time indexes and carrying out calculations with date-time objects can be difficult. For instance, there can be different local formats for the same time period: 7/4/2020 means July 4, 2020 in the US but April 7, 2020 in Europe.

In order to cope with these issues, which were highlighted by the spread of the Internet and globalization processes of the last three decades, efforts have been made to standardize formats, and -while still not truly universal- the *YYYY-mm-dd hh-mm-ss* format (Year, month, day, hour, minute, seconds and maybe fractions of a second) has become pretty much the basic reference. However, **R** still lets you adjust formats to the locale of your choice - two very useful functions:

Sys.localeconv( ) and *Sys.setlocale( )* let you query the system for current settings and change them if needed.

Additionally, there are also different possible format codes in **R** for working with dates, including for example *as.Date, POSIXct, POSIXlt,* and *strptime.* This is not the place to dwell on details concerning these alternatives, but please do take some time to look into them and understand their most important differences. The reason for their existence is basically that you must ensure that date strings are date formats that **R** understands, else they will be processed in ways you probably don't want. Some simple examples should suffice:

```
> notDate <- "2019-07-06"
> class(notDate)
[1] "character"
> d <- as.Date("2019-07-06")
> class(d)
[1] "Date"
> str(d)
Date[1:1], format: "2019-07-06"
```

Now that we're talking fluent date-time language, other functions and operators come to facilitate our work. For instance:

```
> nextw <- d + 2:6     # Next week
> nextw
[1] "2019-07-08" "2019-07-09" "2019-07-10" "2019-07-11"
    "2019-07-12"
> nextw[1]
[1] "2019-07-08"
> weekdays(nextw[1])
[1] "Monday"
> e <- as.Date("2019-12-06")
> e-d
Time difference of 153 days
> as.Date("6 Dec 2019", format = "%d %b %Y")
[1] "2019-12-06"
```

So, with the right format, we can further manipulate these date-time strings and even do some relevant calculations with them (try calculating how old you are in days). *POSIXct* and *POSIXlt* also allow us to do similar things and contain functions to manipulate objects representing calendar dates and times. *POSIXct* is the signed number of seconds since since 00:00:00 Thursday, 1 January 1970. *POSIXlt* corresponds to the more familiar string formats such as May 19, 2019 or 19/05/2019 05:24:39. Some examples of available functions:

```
> Sys.Date()
[1] "2019-07-08"
> Sys.time()
[1] "2019-07-08 11:09:07 CST"
> t1 <- as.POSIXlt(Sys.time())
> t1$hour
[1] 11
> t1$min
[1] 12
> weekdays(t1)
[1] "Monday"
> t2 <- as.POSIXlt(Sys.time())
> months(t2)
[1] "July"
> difftime(t2,t1)
Time difference of 20.52697 secs
```

On the other hand, managing entire *time series* is a neighboring but distinct region of data processing in **R**. As noted earlier, time objects are in this case tied to values produced by measurements or observations on some specific data generating process, whose time indexes also impose a strict and specific ordering of observations.

To illustrate, let's start from this basic distinction between simple sequences and true time series data and build from there. For example, we can generate a simple 24-point linear sequence of numbers and plot it:

```
> plot(1:24, type = 'l',  col = 'blue')
> str(1:24)
int [1:24] 1 2 3 4 5 6 7 8 9 10 ...
```

This is just a straight line with sequence indexes 1...24 along the x-axis. But if you use **R**'s *ts()* (time series) function to define it as a time series object (just like we used *as.Date()* above to define a date-time object), the plot shows the same line of linearly increasing values but now appears chronologically indexed along the x-axis:

```
> tr <- ts(1:24, frequency = 12, start = 2018)
> tr
      Jan Feb Mar Apr May Jun Jul Aug Sep Oct Nov Dec
2018    1   2   3   4   5   6   7   8   9  10  11  12
2019   13  14  15  16  17  18  19  20  21  22  23  24
> plot(tr, col = 'blue')   # Plot it!
> class(tr)
[1] "ts"
> str(tr)
Time-Series [1:24] from 2018 to 2020: 1 2 3 4 5 6 7 8 9 10...
```

The main takeaway is that, not only to correctly plot, but also to be able to use packages and functions that help you with time-series data, you must ensure that the data are understood by **R** as precisely that, time-series data. This is especially true given that many time-series data sources do not index the observations as such. For instance, let's look at US and Japan per capita GDPs by downloading the data from the World Bank.

```
> install.packages("WDI")
> library(WDI)
> gdp <- WDI(country = c("US", "JP"), indicator =
              c("NY.GDP.PCAP.CD"), start=1960, end=2018)
> str(gdp)
'data.frame':           118 obs. of  4 variables:
$ iso2c          : chr  "JP" "JP" "JP" "JP" ...
$ country        : chr  "Japan" "Japan" "Japan" "Japan" ...
$ NY.GDP.PCAP.CD: num  39287 38332 38794 34524 38109 ...
  ..- attr(*, "label")= chr "GDP per capita (current US$)"
$ year           : int  2018 2017 2016 2015 2014 2013 2012
                         2011 2010 2009 ...
```

You can immediately tell that this is not set up as a time series even if it is dated by *year*, which in this case appears as a simple **int**eger and not a true time-series object. Let's extract Japan's per capita, convert it into a true time series and plot the values:

```
> jpgdp <- gdp$NY.GDP.PCAP.CD[gdp$country == "Japan"]
# Reorder - data are ordered most recent first
> jpgdp_ts <- ts(jpgdp[order(length(jpgdp):1)], start =
                 min(gdp$year), frequency = 1)
> str(jpgdp_ts)
Time-Series [1:59] from 1960 to 2018: 479 564 634 718 836 ...
> plot(jpgdp_ts, main="Evolution of Japan's GDP per capita at
        current prices", xlab = 'Year', ylab= "Level")
```

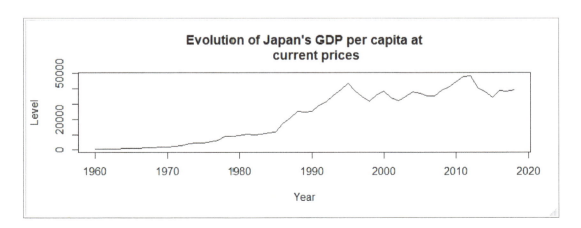

In contrast, the following sequence of instructions loads data that has been already formatted as true time-series data and uses several time-series related functions; culminating in a plot showing the decomposition of the series into its trend, seasonal and random components:

```
> install.packages("AER")
> library(AER)
> data("UKNonDurables")
> str(UKNonDurables)
> tsp(UKNonDurables)              # time series properties
> head(time(UKNonDurables))   # time index
> window(UKNonDurables, end = c(1958,4))
> plot(UKNonDurables)
> decompUKnd <- decompose(UKNonDurables)
> str(decompUKnd)
> plot(decompUKnd)
```

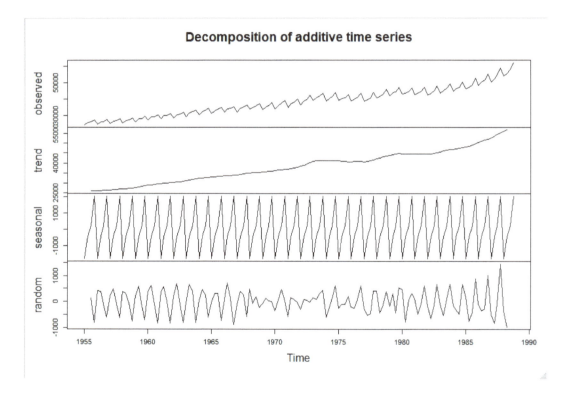

A final warning – *ggplot2( )* takes a dataframe as input, so to plot your time series you must adjust correspondingly. For example, to use Japan's per capita GDP you must use the *as.data.frame( )* function and proceed like:

```
> dates <- as.Date(min(gdp$year): max(gdp$year))
> jg <- as.data.frame(cbind(jpgdp_ts,dates))
```

```
> str(jg)
'data.frame':   59 obs. of  2 variables:
 $ jpgdp_ts: num   473 564 634 718 836 ...
 $ dates    : num   1950 1961 1962 1963 1964 ...
> ggplot(data = jg, aes(x = dates, y = jpgdp_ts)) +
        geom_line(color = "#00AFBB", size = 1)   + labs(x =
        "Years", y = "GDP per capita")
# Plot a subset of the data
> ss <- subset(jg, dates > 2000)
> ggplot(data = ss, aes(x = dates, y = jpgdp_ts)) +
        geom_line(color = "#004E07", size = 1)   + labs(x =
        "More recent years", y = "GDP per capita")
```

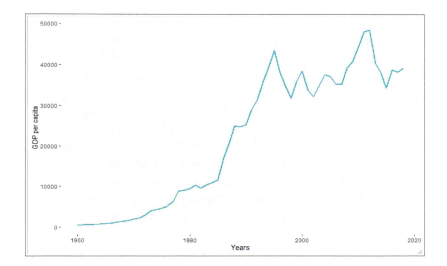

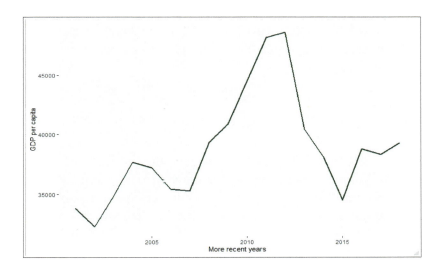

Programming and Control structures

Programming - in a broad sense - is nothing more than the art and science of being able to communicate with a computer's hardware effectively. You tell the computer what you want to do, following very strict grammatical rules or *syntax*, plus how to get back the results (numbers, text, images or combinations of these) in a comprehensible way; and if everything goes well your cybernetic dialog will be joyful.

Modern computers, operating systems and software programs have advanced very much in the way of automating and easing this interface between humans and microcircuits. It hasn't been always like this, and early programmers had to deal almost directly with the hardware using *machine language*. With the advent of *high level languages* (such as **R**) programmers can almost speak English with the computer - the operating system and firmware translate,[9] so to speak, semi-natural language commands to machine language which in turn speaks to the computer's microcircuits; which carry out some process (like printing) or some computation whose results are translated back to 'human' and conveyed back to the programmer staring at the screen.

Therefore, at least in this broad sense, you've been programming all along as you have progressed through this walk-through. When you write at **R**'s prompt something like

```
> mult <- 2*3    # Remember?
> mult
[1] 6
```

you're using **R** to tell the computer to compute the result of multiplying two times three and to hold the integer value 6 somewhere in a memory location which you will refer to as *mult*. Similarly, you can ask the computer to hold some text (characters, strings) in memory that represent the English words "Hello world", and calculate the total number of characters that make up that string using the bulit-in function *nchar()*:

---

9 *Compile* or *interpret* in technical jargon.

```
> nchar("Hello world")   # The space counts as a character
[1] 11
```

The word 'programming' is however mostly reserved for writing a series of commands at the editor (expressions and statements) which carry out a specific task. A particular combination of commands which solve a given problem is called an *algorithm*, so it is perfectly possible for several algorithms to solve the same problem. Which is the best? Well, it all depends - sometimes you have to decide, for instance, between accuracy and speed, so there can be trade-offs in this ranking.

In any case, a very simple program - printing "Hello world!" - can be easily implemented in **R** by going to the main menu and pressing **File**, **New File**, **R Script**. The Editor tab will show an empty page initially called *Untitled1** which you can rename, for example, *Hello world.R* (very creative) by pressing on the **Save** icon and choosing where to keep it.

```
Untitled1* ×                                                    Run      Source ▾
  1  # Program to use the print() function
  2  print("Hello World!")
  3  |
```

You can then select the whole program or part of it and click on the **Run** icon

```
Hello world.R ×                                                 Run      Source ▾
  1  # Program to use the print() function
  2  print("Hello World!")
  3  |
```

and at the console you should see "Hola mundo!" (just kidding):

```
# Program to use the print() function
> print("Hello World!")
[1] "Hello World!"
```

Believe it or not this is a full program. The algorithm is simply to use the built-in function *print( )* to accomplish our goal. Notice that the comment (the line beginning with #) adds nothing to the algorithm - it is there only for documentation purposes, which in a large program can be indispensable.

Now let's be more daring and write a program to convert Fahrenheit temperatures to Celsius. This (the algorithm) could go something like

```
# Program - Fahrenheit to Celsius
F <- 85
Celsius <- (F - 32) * (5/9)
Celsius

> F <- 85
> Celsius <- (F - 32) * (5/9)
> Celsius
[1] 29.44444
```

Nice! Now I know that 85 F is 29.4 Celsius. But now I want to try 32 F, or 75 F or 100 F, etc. The problem is that I must run the program every time I change the value of the variable F, which in the worst case could involve turning the computer on, opening RStudio, loading the program and running it just to see how hot 90 F is on the Celsius scale this very sunny afternoon. Well, if I think about it, that really shouldn't be a problem - that's exactly what I wanted the program to do, wasn't it?

This problem of not clearly specifying what you want out of a program creeps up in almost all programming situations, even in apparently very simple ones. Maybe what I really wanted was some sort of table I can pin to my cork board or refrigerator where I can quickly look up and visualize conversions without all the aforementioned hassle. To do this, I will enclose my conversion algorithm in a function I shall name *F_to_Celsius( )*, which will take as sole parameter the F degrees reading, and then print a table of conversions to Celsius from reasonable year-round Fahrenheit temperature readings in my locale, mentally interpolating for in-between values if I need to:

```
# Program - Fahrenheit to Celsius

F_to_Celsius <- function(F) {
  Celsius <- (F - 32) * (5/9)
  return(Celsius)
}

reasonableFs <- c(32,40,50,60,70,80,90)
```

```
conversions <- F_to_Celsius(reasonableFs)

sprintf("%3.1f F is equivalent to %3.1f degrees Celsius ",
reasonableFs, conversions) # Format function - look it up!

[1] "32.0 F is equivalent to 0.0 degrees Celsius"
[2] "40.0 F is equivalent to 4.4 degrees Celsius"
[3] "50.0 F is equivalent to 10.0 degrees Celsius"
[4] "60.0 F is equivalent to 15.6 degrees Celsius"
[5] "70.0 F is equivalent to 21.1 degrees Celsius"
[6] "80.0 F is equivalent to 26.7 degrees Celsius"
[7] "90.0 F is equivalent to 32.2 degrees Celsius"
```

My *F_to_Celsius( )* function *returns* a Celsius equivalent (you must tell your functions to *return* something [10]); and even if it apparently returns only one number at a time it actually maps nicely to the *reasonableFs* vector with no problem at all (**R** is very good at this) and yields the *conversions* vector, which may be used to output a formatted table.

But now, as often happens, it occurs to me that I can get more out of this program than what I initially imagined. For example, the program could tell me (as if I didn't know!) the qualitative feel of each level of Celsius temperatures - '*0.0 degrees Celsius is cold*', or something to the effect.

So now I will need **R**'s help to do two things - **repeat** an examination of each temperature (one by one) and **decide** (according to my subjective scale) which temperatures are cool, pleasant or hot. It turns out that these two actions, *repeat* and *decide*, are fundamental constructs of every programming language out there; be it **R**, Python, Java, Kotlin, Go or whatever. The other fundamental construct, **sequence**, completes this crucial set of constructs and just refers to the order in which instructions are executed. For example, most languages execute line by line from top to bottom of a program, but some languages include a *goto* statement that allows the execution to jump to some other line - this practice is almost universally discouraged because of the 'spaghetti code' it often produces.[11] So in **R** just think 'sequential execution'.

Going back to the other two constructs, **decision** or **selection** statements make the program fork in one direction or another depending on some condition: '*if ebook title price is between $2.99 to $9.99 royalty is 70%, else royalty is only 35%.*' Statements starting with *if* and *else if* are typical of selection and decision-making in programs.

---

10 If there are no explicit *returns* the value of the last evaluated expression is returned by default.
11 **R** has a *callCC( )* function - call with current continuation - which is used to perform non-local exits but is seldom used.

In the **repeat** or **iteration** department **R** has *for-loops*, *while loops*, and *repeat-loops*. For example, print the squares of the first 10 natural numbers: *'for a number i in the range 1:10 print(i^2)'*.

You can break out of loops with *'break'* and jump to the next iteration with *'next'*. Repetition causes one or more program statements (*i^2* in the preceding example) to be processed repeatedly until some end condition is met (10 times in this case).

As an aside, always remember that there are many resources in **R** to iterate without using loops, which tend to be computationally expensive.

Vectorization and *mappings*, mentioned previously, are among the most used alternatives to loops – if you recall the Kilos to pounds example early in the book, it is entirely possible to do it with a *for* loop, converting Kilos to pounds one by one. However, the vectorized solution that was presented there is much simpler and faster. Loops are presented because they are fundamental constructs and because in a diversity of situations they are the only or best alternative.

In any case, unless you're facing a really big data processing task, the efficiency of *for* loops vs alternatives is not going to make a huge difference.

Let's not be pedantic – until you get comfortable with **R**'s fancy vectorizations or mappings just go ahead and use whatever *repeat* construct does the job. You will get better at it with time.

Going back to our problem, following is a simple program to convert from F degrees to C degrees and to qualify the result according to ranges of temperatures.

The *for* loop does the iterating over all values of F readings, which are converted one-by-one to C by calling the *F_to_Celsius( )* function on each pass.

The *if* statement with nested *else if* statements lets me select among alternative temperature ranges and tag a subjective descriptor for each one, while at the same time printing the results to a table.

Note that braces (*{ }*) are used as separators for blocks or sections of code and that the overweight *print* statements are just doing a lot of formatting work. Try to follow the basic logic and the role played by *sequence*, *selection* and *iteration*:

```
# Program - Fahrenheit to Celsius with descriptors

F_to_Celsius <- function(F) {
  Celsius <- (F - 32) * (5/9)
  return(Celsius)
}

reasonableFs <- c(32,40,50,60,70,80,90)

for (i in reasonableFs) {   # i is called the iterator
  temp <- F_to_Celsius(i)   # i passes each F to the function
  if (temp < 10) {
    print(paste(i, "F is", format(temp, digits=3,
        nsmall=2),"C - Cold"))
  } else if (temp >= 10 && temp <= 18) {
      print(paste(i, "F is", format(temp, digits=3,
          nsmall=2),"C - Cool"))
  } else if (temp >= 18 && temp <= 27) {
      print(paste(i, "F is", format(temp, digits=3,
          nsmall=2),"C - Pleasant"))
  } else {
      print(paste(i, "F is", format(temp, digits=3,
          nsmall=2),"C - Hot"))
  }
}

[1] "32 F is 0.00 C - Cold"
[1] "40 F is 4.44 C - Cold"
[1] "50 F is 10.00 C - Cool"
[1] "60 F is 15.56 C - Cool"
[1] "70 F is 21.11 C - Pleasant"
[1] "80 F is 26.67 C - Pleasant"
[1] "90 F is 32.22 C - Hot
```

Even if this is a very basic example and introduction to programming, in essence this is basically all there is to it. You have data (such as "Hello, world!", b <- 3, a vector of temperature readings, many volumes of text or a big bank's database with millions of records) which you want to process in some way. To do it, you give instructions sequentially, make decisions and select paths based on certain conditions and, if necessary, iterate or loop through a series of steps until you achieve a specific outcome.

In this process, as we've said from the very start, you can create user-defined functions[12] and even write your very own packages to better organize and

---

12 In technical jargon **R** is primarily a *functional* programming language. Other languages are mostly Object Oriented languages, using 'objects' to encapsulate and reuse code; and still other languages implement a mix of different programming paradigms.

reuse your code, especially in long, complex programs. But it is not absolutely necessary - you can do anything that is computable using the three fundamental constructs, even if your code is messy and repetitive (not recommended).

There are many excellent books, tutorials and online courses on programming for **R**, or on any programming language for that matter. Hopefully, this walk-through will motivate you to go further in that direction.

Resources

Data

https://registry.opendata.aws/

https://misfra.me/2016/04/09/tsdb-list/

https://datarepository.wolframcloud.com/

https://www.datasciencecentral.com/profiles/blogs/a-plethora-of-data-set-repositories

https://knoema.com/

http://archive.ics.uci.edu/ml/index.php

https://www.datasciencecentral.com/profiles/blogs/great-github-list-of-public-data-sets

https://www.data.gov/

https://data.worldbank.org/

Graphics and plots

https://www.r-graph-gallery.com/

https://www.rdocumentation.org/packages/graphics/versions/3.6.1

https://vcg.informatik.uni-rostock.de/~ct/timeviz/timeviz.html

https://www.tidyverse.org/

Other R distributions and IDEs

https://mran.microsoft.com/open

https://www.microsoft.com/en-us/sql-server/machinelearningserver

https://rkward.kde.org/

https://jstaf.github.io/2018/03/25/atom-ide.html

https://docs.microsoft.com/en-us/power-bi/desktop-r-ide

R language

https://www.r-bloggers.com/

https://www.rdocumentation.org/

https://www.statmethods.net/index.html

https://www.r-graph-gallery.com/

https://cran.r-project.org/

RStudio

https://www.rstudio.com/

https://support.rstudio.com/hc/en-us

Alphabetical Index

About the Author

Hermann M. Hess is an artist, economist and data scientist. He holds a PhD in Economics from the University of Pittsburgh and has successfully completed all the coursework in the Data Science Specialization from the Coursera-Johns Hopkins online course. He is also a painter who has participated in several collective art shows and currently displays his artwork in 'real' galleries and online galleries, receiving an *Artist Recognition - Artist featured in a collection* from Saatchi Art.

He enjoys teaching economics and data science; and shares with the family a predilection for music, movies, soccer, American football and dining out on weekends.

The author will be happy to hear from you at *hermann.m.hess@gmail.com*